Lineage of Rain

Lineage of Rain

Janel Pineda

Haymarket Books
Chicago, IL

Published in 2021 by
Haymarket Books
P.O. Box 180165
Chicago, IL 60618
773-583-7884
www.haymarketbooks.org
info@haymarketbooks.org

ISBN: 978-1-64259-527-7

Distributed to the trade in the US through Consortium Book Sales
and Distribution (www.cbsd.com) and internationally through Ingram
Publisher Services International (www.ingramcontent.com).

This book was published with the generous support of Lannan Founda-
tion and Wallace Action Fund.

Special discounts are available for bulk purchases by organizations and
institutions. Please call 773-583-7884 or email info@haymarketbooks.
org for more information.

Cover artwork by Kiara Aileen Machado.
Cover design by Jamie Kerry.

Library of Congress Cataloging-in-Publication data is available.

10 9 8 7 6 5 4 3 2 1

Contents

IN ANOTHER LIFE

The war never happened but somehow you and I
    still exist. Like obsidian,
we know only the memory of lava
    and not the explosion that created

us. Forget the gunned-down church, the burning
    flesh, the cabbage soup.
There is no bus. There is no border. There is no blood.
    There are

only sweet corn fields and mango skins. The turquoise
    house and clotheslines.
A heaping plate of pasteles and curtido waiting to be
    disappeared into our bellies.

In this life, our people are not things of silences
    but whole worlds bursting
into breath. Everywhere, there are children. Playing
    freely, clothed and clean.

Mozote does not mean massacre and flowers bloom
    in every place shoes are
left behind. My name still means truth, this time
    in a language my mouth recognizes,

in a language I know how to speak. My grandmother is
    still a storyteller although I am
not a poet. In this life, I do not have to be. This poem
    somehow still exists. It is told

in my mother's voice and she makes hurt dissolve like honey
    in hot water, manzanilla

warming the throat. You and I do not find each other
          on another continent, grasping

at each other's necks in search of home. We meet in a mercado,
          my arms overflowing
with mamey and anonas, and together we wash them
          in riverwater. We watch sunset fall over

a land we call our own and do not fear its taking.
          I bite into the fruit, mouth sucking
seed from substance, pulling its veins from between my teeth.
          Our laughter echoes

from inside the cave, one we are free to step outside of.
          We do not have to hide here.
We do not have to hide anywhere. A torogoz flies past my face
          and I do not fear its flapping.

I.

RAIN

I begin here:
kneeling by Tana's bedside
begging for a story.

> *¡cuénteme un cuento, Tana*
> *cuénteme un cuento!*

Tana waters my hair,
combs it back
into a tight braid.

> *Va pues, bicha.*
> *Venite aquí.*

Before words erupt,
a roar of her laughter
like miel; Tana bursts

with carcajadas newly-hatched
and tells of cafetales
of serpents and machetes

of the blistering feel
of sun, of the taste of dirt
on tongue, of men swallowed
by earth de pura vergüenza.

> *¿me entendiste, cipota?*
> *sí, I nod. sí, Tana.*

///

the first time I ask Tana
why she left El Salvador,
me dice: *porque allá mucho llueve.*

for weeks, Tana watched sky fall
to earth from bus windows. she held on tightly
to herself and the thought of mi mami,
borders away and alone somewhere en la capital.

no hay tiempo para esas babosadas, she thought
wiping her eye-made rain away.
Tana massaged her bloody feet into silence,
her throat aching for just one sip.

///

for years, I am afraid of rain.
I am six years old and praying for sun.
when rainfall begins, I run
indoors, get caught by a teacher
in a cafeteria corner, crying.
I am six years old and believe
every time it rains, it is time to flee.
I am six years old and afraid
of being left behind.
I am six years old and my blood remembers
what it feels like to leave
a whole homeland behind.

///

a Salvadoran woman once wrote:
our poetry has never had the luxury
of being enamored with the moon.

perhaps this is why all my poems
are about the sun, about coming from
women who have survived

by chasing it, women who go
only where the light will feed
them, women who leave
the second they suspect
a flood.

SOUTH GATE FOURTH OF JULY

Our mothers declare our freedom
      y salimos corriendo, knees ashed
by firework dust, pockets filled

      with pop-its. We spell stories
con sparklers, throw cohetes at our sisters'
      ankles, then run to hide

behind the apartment dumpster,
      knowing they'll get us back soon.
Inside our home, fingers foil

      for the LAX Tacos stacked
on the table. We soak them in limes
      then bite rábanosly, salsa running

sticky down our forearms. Chestnut Avenue
      pours with kids, our older siblings
ready with packs of Mentos and Coke

      to make the fireworks go higher.
They huddle around to light the flame then skid
      away. Hoodied figures in basketball shorts

flock to the curb, to watch the fire
      work its way into the southeast sky,
neon sparks illuminating our faces.

FIFTH GRADE SHOW AND TELL

El Salvador
is a country
too small to stand
out on the map
it is 8,124 square miles
of cobblestone roads
cafetales and greenery
leading up
to the volcanic skyline
and the way
the bitter skin
of the mamey
leaves your tongue
with the itchy
burn that is
cured only
by its sweet
insides and how
navidad really is
the most feliz
time of all
with the metralleta
fireworks
setting palm trees
on fire
in the night heat
of diciembre
and the two
american girls
wondering
why the hell
no one's

called 9-1-1
another day
el chaparro
goes to el centro
and orders
un mango cumbia
sucking the lime
and pressing
the cool bottle
to his forehead
after the never-ending
day of work
and finally
comes home
to his esposa
who gives him
everything, no matter
how tired
she is too
she has the plate
of frijoles
and queso duro
ready
with the café
just right
she is always
just right
so she takes
a moment
for herself
kicks her feet up
on the hamaca
and sings
that song
from her favorite

novela
she sings
that song
so loud
I hear her
from my room
further up
the continent

HOW ENGLISH CAME TO GRANDMA

Beatles songs blared
from the small radio in her kitchen

& twenty-something-year-old Elba
danced to "A Hard Day's Night,"
singing English into existence in
a place it never should have arrived.

Like a work of brujería, English
enamored her
into thinking the US   perfect.

For grandma, everything americano
was soaked in English and she
wanted to bathe in that language's
ocean, no matter how bloody
she pretended it didn't look.

Inglés la conquistó a pura paja
stuck its tongue down her throat
then bewitched her feet to follow it.

Grandma tells me she fled
in search of it, traced
its footprints up the isthmus
to Los Estados Unidos
the obvious place to go
the place where everybody ended
up, whether they wanted to or not

'cause, come on!
where else would they go
but to the place to which they all
belonged? No,

I don't mean they belonged there
I mean they belonged *to.*

ALL THIS TO TELL YOU: GRANDMA STILL DOES NOT SPEAK ENGLISH

She tried wrestling it once
but it twisted her tongue.

    So instead she clings
    to "Grandma"
    and never "Abuela"

    her *ay lob jus*   instead of *te quiero*

    her Beatles lyrics

her thick *jes mahm*'s
and *rright agüey, mahm*

    from her jobs cleaning houses
    in *wudlahn Heel*   *paz á Dína*

        sometimes even *beh-ver-lé Heel*

her Spanglish

    and her *ay so sori*'s.

Because if she knows anything about English,

    it's how much that language demands
    her to apologize.

THE ASSESSMENT FORM ASKS
ABOUT MY ANXIETY

Let me begin with birds.
        Brown wings butterfly-kissing
my eyelids open. Yellow chicks
        in a child's hands, squeezed
out of youthful joy. The marshmallowed
        peeps I believed their corpses.

I could tell you about the rain,
        how quickly I was convinced
it would drown me if I let it.
        Every winter I'd press my hot face
to classroom glass, rolled-up sweatshirt
        sleeves wet and sticky.

Or else I could tell you a story
        about hunger,
the salt of your sweat a seasoning
        —spoonfuls of dirt
crackling on your tongue
        then unsettling your stomach.

It wouldn't be a story I've lived
        but it is still a story of mine,
this muscle memory
        of scavenging for scraps,
the insistence to prepare
        to run, to hide, to flee.

I could tell you about the men,
        their hands, their laughter

—but only if you promise to believe me.
        I could tell you about
not being believed,
        though I'd rather not.

I could give up and throw
        some big keywords at you.
War. Migration. Diaspora.
        Don't all the traumas of my blood
begin there? But if they're too heavy
        for your heart, let me go back to the birds:

their flutter a fury inside my chest,
        ribcaged flight fighting
to be freed. My panic is no more
        than their song-turned-screech,
what happens when a free and fragile thing
        is forced to survive.

WHEN THE DEATH SQUADS COME

They will come as they have always come: in broad daylight, at your door, grinning. Each knock the echo of a wound. They will take you from the classroom, each child's tears a river leading back to the parent who lies somewhere in the sand. They will find you just before dusk. At the 6 p.m. church service. When they are done with you, only shoes remain. You will run from them on foot. On the bus that can hardly be called a bus. On all your life savings and then some. If you make it to the false-promise land, you are safe. For now. If not, you will hide away. In the caves. In another's name—yours in flames. In the parts of el campo you think they will not dare go looking for you. When they come, you will warn the children, reminding them: *we've been through this before.* Some will live to tell the tale. Some will tell it. Or else, the death squads are already in your house. Turning the hamaca into a sinister thing, beer bottle from your fridge in hand. They have just come to ask some questions, they say. Questions that cannot be solved. They ask your name. To ask your name is to ask your life. You do not have another's to borrow. In the kitchen, the kettle's screech mirrors your insides. You wonder which will come first. The coffee or the bullet. The sun bright on your cheek-bones, coffee burning your tongue. *What a shame*, some will say. *What a shame. The brightest mind with a bullet in the brain.*

TÍO TOÑO IS READY TO DIE

over coffee and tamales.
He almost, but doesn't
admit this to me.

Hija—aquí, tené,
hands quaking as coffee
flows from a red mug.

He sits down slowly,
nudges the sugar
across the table.

He smiles.
I smile back.
I am happy to be here

with him, Mami's sole story
-teller after Tana left
north. We sit in the house

of the black gecko's kiss;
rainfall begins
and so do my questions.

                    *

The word "war" does not leave
his lips, but lives
in how his head hangs

a downward gaze
remembering when a uniformed
man pushed him onto ledge

shoved gun in spine
and asked if he believed

in God
            or in government

in good
            or in gore.

Tío Toño bowed his head
in prayer, waited for bullet—

Good God   Good   God   Good   God

—got blessing instead.

In the distance, a voice called out.
Si le disparás al señor ese,
vos serás el próximo que muere.

                    *

The tamal pisque disappears
in his toothless chew as he raises
his head for the first time in our meal.

I knew that boy
the one who saved me.
That boy was once

a good boy
a God boy
not a government boy.

He lets out a sigh.
His whole body trembles.
I ask what I can do for his pain.

Tío Toño tells me
he won't ask God
to save him this time

—no, not again.

WHEN THE MEN COME LOOKING

I turn siguanaba cloaked in river
blood, face of horse or hair or hell. I strip
down to my slip and wait to catch them in
my snare. Arms long and lasso-like, my dark
yellowed eyes lure them in. Dizzying in
a wink. Fingers extend, wiry, showing
off this manicure de mugre, my nails
bite into monstrous men and make them mad.
They ask for it, their deaths—something about how
they walked into their wives fist-first, or lost
their hands up someone's skirt. I come to them
dream-like, at first, tell them to find me at
the finca's edge. They always come looking
for me. As if they don't know what's coming.

II.

FELLOWSHIP APPLICATION

The Commission's criteria includes:
(1) Ability to be Tokenized
(2) Strength of Migrant Mentality
(3) Diplomatic Disposition
(4) Self-care or private health insurance.

(The fourth category was added in response to excessive
complaints about mental health.)

*

Recite your trauma in iambic pentameter
then pirouette back into palatable prose.
Remind the reviewers of their privilege but not
of their guilt; remember, it is your job to recognize
and respond to the need for representation.

You must be prepared to excel on the Commission's annual panels
but not necessarily in daily life. Be sure to mention your parents'
labor, your siblings' aching bellies. Scholarship awards
are based on generational access, but for the sake of your brown
faces on our website, the Commission makes exceptions.

Give thanks to the empire for the opportunity to be
considered. Close your essays politely,
with a dream you dream they find you worthy of.

HOW ENGLISH CAME TO ME

It made its home
                              hovering
                    around my body
the first four years of my life.
Sometimes, it tired
                              and rested
     in my shadow
                    trailed slimy red and sticky but
     always   waited
          knew my hatred would pass
               that I'd find my way to its lap.
                                        Soon
          I'd rest my head on its shoulder
curl up against fragmented bone
               and let it dig its hands around my spine.

     English was patient   because it knew
     it would win   in this country
                              I wouldn't
          be able to resist much longer.

          Sometimes I can still hear
          English's cackle
          when at four years old
          I proclaimed:

                    ¡No me hable así!
          ¡Yo no hablo inglés y nunca lo hablaré!

                    *

26

Weeks later   in kindergarten
I let English reign over
                          my body
    let myself soak   in its liquid power.

*

I dizzied myself in this winding river   made its waters the
                language I tell stories in
    built a home in its classes   declared a major in its body
chased it up the Thames   to the world's oldest English-speaking
            university   tossed away spanish
        reserved it for Saturdays   sometimes
    or visits to grandma's   and even now   the only spanish that
            lives in this poem is faint   memory
        the words of a younger   braver   self

*

            and I'm afraid
            'cause I bet
            English is sitting
            somewhere in this room
            clutching its stomach

            rolling over in laughter
            at how I typed these words
            sometimes first in spanish
            then backspaced my return to English.

BECAUSE PAPI DROVE LINCOLNS

For our living, we had:
    signed Beatles records
                leftover eggplant parmesan
                from the Beverly Hills restaurants
winter fruit baskets
    & the blessings of a hundred-dollar tip.

When Papi's clients left behind their belongings in the car, we had:
    a Nikon D300   brand new Beats $675 Armani flats
& Coach wallets too small
                to hold the song of centavos in our pockets.

We kids knew what each client preferred—whether it was
        Essentia   or Core Perfect pH alkaline water
a supply of Red Vines   lemon slices   or Diet Coke
        ready in the armrest.

We longed for the days   when Papi's clients departed
from their holiday homes   & housekeepers emptied fridges
        into the trunk of Papi's town car:
a whole aisle of Whole Foods leftovers   Tetris-packed inside.

We learned that crops are only seasonal
    for those who have to grow them
                knew the elite could spare
                what we couldn't afford

Still, when I left LA, I knew to order the Sicilian Pistachio flavor
    of Van Leeuwen Artisan Ice Cream
knew to talk Stones or Springsteen with my white friends' parents

knew to mention the Huntington Gardens at my first Oxford dinner
  where a professor asked me why the libraries in LA
  allow such "unseemly" people   to enter them

        where he wondered aloud how I "managed"
        to be sitting at the same table as him.

TO THE ELDEST DAUGHTER

because she remembered
to unfreeze the chicken
steam the arroz
wash the dishes
and prepare snacks
for the kids
after picking them up
from school,
dinner was
always half-ready
by the time
mami got home
from her twelve-hour
hospital shift
and I'd emerge quietly
from the books
I drowned myself in
those days
when I took for granted
the things she
inevitably sacrificed:
time with friends
the basketball team
her own homework
a childhood
learning to play
the cello

instead, she helped mami
raise the rest of us
while I wrote
she changed diapers

washed the cars
opened the windows
mopped the floors
took the heat
when I broke
the family camera
pulled me aside
and scolded me
for not understanding
our parents couldn't
afford the fancy
summer programs
I begged for
and still, I'm sure
she stayed up helping
the summer mami decided
to sell burritos
every evening
after work
so they could pay
for me to go write poems
in Tennessee

years of my jet-setting
big dreaming
sleeping soundly
knowing she was
home doing everything
that needed doing
and still she drove
six days
cross-country
alone
to watch me
descend

Old West's steps
graduation cap
and all,
the string of roses
she spent all night sewing
draped over
my neck—

oh, hermana
I bow to you
now as I did then,
wreathed
by the grace
of every goodness
you have given.

IMAGINED PORTRAIT OF MY FATHER AS ARCHITECT

Forehead lines fade. The red of his eyes returns
to the road. No longer migrant, Dad drives himself
only. Still wears a white collar. A man of maps,

he lays out his plans on the dining room table
when he steps inside our home, singing
loudly. Unlike the under-breath tones

of the other life, here his song is a belted building
we all chime in to help assemble. With hands
free from steering wheel, Dad's arms stretch

outward, point to the burnt sienna roofs of his own
design. Dad does not move musicians, but everyone
moves to music. Papi is still pillar, but not patriarch.

Mami manda todavía. The two cook together,
all the tías and tíos and little primitos a crowd
spilling over into the garden of frutas outside.

Papi plays the accordion, has time
to teach us kids how to master it. We sing
together at the lakeside house he built us

all our voices booming sin vergüenza.

BEFORE THE INTERVIEW

Little sister's hands tug
at my hair, mapping
her faith in me into my scalp

as she braids colochos into crown, holy
around my head, then secures
with bobby pins, twisting my bun twice

and then again until a grin appears
wide across her face, teeth brave, bold
like our blood, her eyes beam at me

as I sit on the living room floor, trembling
the morning of the interview and her hands
still tug, taming the mechas of my mind

as she declares me a particular kind
of royalty, a particular kind of world-changer,
turns and says *Oooh. You got this, hermana!!*

*

and thank God, I do—
thanks to my little brother's prayers, which he sends
upwards from la gran mesa in the kitchen

last night's homework still strewn across it,
along with the breakfast Mami made
which I am too nervous to eat, so instead

34

before heading to school, my brother sits
calmly in his light, head folded into his palms
in prayer, he begs: *Diosito—please, please*

let my sister have her dreams, let my sister have her dreams
        please God she works so hard
en el nombre de tu hijo amado Cristo Jesús, amén.

*

Big sister waits for me in the car, drives
me to the consulate, then around the block again
until I am brave enough to step out the car

she holds the hands she painted carefully
the night before, as she polished
their nails, repeating: *You're gonna get it sis. You always do.*

like she knows something I don't
believe yet, something I am still learning
to hold. She holds it for me now, shakes her head:

Naw, sis. How could they possibly not choose you?

WHEN THE CALL FINALLY COMES

What joy to be surrounded by siblings—to exclaim

> *"we're going to England, we're going to England!"*

as we cry together in the car en route to Target

> where we shop for the most luxurious of things:

> reduced-price sweaters

Hot Cheeto Puffs (the most coveted of chips)

> peppermint soap

> hardcover books

a giant plush unicorn my little sister stuffs into the cart.

> We indulge every sweetness &

I repeat the words of Lucille Clifton in my head,

> like I had done every day before the interview:

except this time *my one hand holding tight*

> not only *my other hand,* but my siblings'.

ALL THIS TO SHOW YOU

How I take English
by its bloodied shoulders
dissolving its body
into its own soris
until it offers its wallet
to pay for my flat
by the river
where I spend
months learning love
finding ways
to forgive
this tongue
its treachery
this language
once monstrous
made wholly
my own.

INSTEAD OF PRODUCING

papaya needed peeling
needed its skin slit

along its sides, to release
the bitter of its milk

needed to spend hours
sweetening in the sun

needed to be cut open
for its seeds needed saving

to turn salve for the stomach
and its flesh needed time

to turn a deeper orange
which needed to be served

into bowl and be bitten
needed to nourish

the body whose hair
needed braiding and

the body whose song
needed listening to and

the body who had not had
a thing to eat yet and

the body who had spent
all day tending

to patients, the body
whose legs needed

stretching, whose feet
needed another's fingers

to walk along their soles
until the aching stopped,

the body whose arms
kneaded flour, water, salt

because bread needed
to become

needed to rest
so it could rise

and bake
and once ready

bread needed
to be centered

needed the company
of other foods

needed a family
to gather around

and behold its being,
bowing their heads

in thanks
for this blessing

& IT IS GREEN

I have seen the future & it is
green. close your eyes & inhala
onetwothreefour exhala.

open them now and see with me:

mami and I still alive
viejitas together, rocking gently
on the porch of a wood-framed house
in a future worthy of our joy.

mami's hair mid-length, loose silver
over her shoulders, mis colochos
tangled back into a single braid.

we are mid-laughter, her brown
-spotted hands and my own
hold each other
in the way of the newborn's grip:
hand wrapped around a single finger

—a sign of a flesh claimed as its own.
mami's eyes glisten green.
with her toothless smile,
mami grins so big
she'll save the world
all over again.

Acknowledgments

Abrazos y todo mi amor to my people, who helped make these poems possible, who reflected back my light in the moments I needed it most. This book is for, and because of, you.

To my parents—todo, todo lo que soy se lo debo a ustedes. Thank you for teaching me, for guiding me, for giving me this beautiful life. To my sisters, Priscilla and Natalie, for your love and care; to my brother Danny, for being the first reader of this book. Gracias a Tana, por sus cuentos, su cariño, sus enseñanzas. Gracias a Grandma Elba, por todo su valor y sus esfuerzos. To tía Dee Dee, for always seeing me, and to Uncle Ron, who wanted the first signed copy but left us before he could get it. Los amo a todos.

To my Salvis and Central American community, especially my CISPES fam, fellow Radical Roots delegates, La Piscucha editorial team, and the intergenerational working group for La Cherada: it is an honor to learn with and from you, to imagine, dream, and build with you. A mi familia en El Salvador, especialmente Tío Jimmy, muchas gracias por apoyarme durante mis visitas a El Salvador.

To eXiled Poetry Society, especially Alejandro Heredia and Hayat Rasul, for teaching me to write in truth and fire. To my Winter Tangerine fall workshop cohort. To the Macondo Writers' Workshop, especially Joy Castro, Kay Ulanday Barrett, Alana Hinojosa, Saúl Hernández, Xelena Gonzalez, and so many others, for your encouragement and inspiration. Mil gracias a los poetas del V Festival de Poesía Amada Libertad, por unas de las experiencias mas bellas de compartir poesía— especialmente le doy las gracias a Alberto López Serrano, Josué Andrés Moz, Cynthia Guardado, Betún Valerio, Mariel Damián, y Pablo Siguenza. To my literary community in London, especially Nathalie Teitler, Bridge Writers Collective, and Maura Dooley.

To féi hernandez, for seeing the sun in me always, for learning and growing with me all these years. To Antonio López, for your love and care with these poems, for your ceaseless encouragement throughout this journey, for your infinite faith in me and this book.

To Ariana Benson, Sarah Yerima, Maia Elsner, Alan Chazaro, Willy Palomo, and Javier Zamora, for their generous eyes on this manuscript. To Claire Celestin, Attiya Latif, Abdiel López, Mergitu Yadeto, and so many others, for your friendship throughout this process. Gratitude also to these writers for their support: Christopher Soto, Francisco Aragón, Jo'Van O'Neal, José Angel Araguz, Allison Deegan, Xochitl-Julisa Bermejo, among others.

To José Olivarez, for being such a generous and supportive editor, and for believing in my poems in the first place. To Maya Marshall and Haymarket Books for bringing this book to fruition. To Kiara Aileen Machado, for creating the stunningly beautiful artwork that graces this cover.

Finally, thank you to the editors of the following journals and anthologies, for including selected poems from this chapbook in their publications: *wildness*, *LitHub*, *PANK*, *Latino Book Review*, *Wandering Song: Central American Writing in the U.S.*, *Accolades: A Women Who Submit Anthology*, and *BreakBeat Poets Vol. 4: LatiNext*.

About the Author

LUZ MARÍA CASTILLO

JANEL PINEDA (b. 1996 Los Angeles, CA) is a Salvadoran poet and educator. A first-generation college graduate, she earned a BA in English from Dickinson College, where she was a Posse Scholar. Pineda has performed her poetry internationally in both English and Spanish, and been published in *LitHub, PANK, BreakBeat Poets, Vol. 4: LatiNext,* and *Wandering Song: Central American Writing in the U.S.,* among others. She is a part of the editorial team that founded *La Piscucha Magazine,* a multilingual arts, literature, and culture magazine created by Salvadoran writers. Since her involvement with the 2018 Radical Roots Delegation, Pineda is also a member of the Committee in Solidarity with the People of El Salvador (CISPES). As a Marshall Scholar, Pineda holds an MA in Creative Writing and Education from Goldsmiths, University of London.

CPSIA information can be obtained
at www.ICGtesting.com
Printed in the USA
JSHW021023050921
18442JS00002B/4